BLESSED NAMES

8

BLESSED NAMES

WHY WAS HE NAMED AS-SADIQ (A)?

WRITTEN BY:
KISA KIDS PUBLICATIONS

Please recite a Fātiḥah for the marḥūmīn
of the Rangwala family, the sponsors of this book.

All proceeds from the sale of this book
will be used to produce more educational resources.

Dedication

This book is dedicated to the beloved Imām of our time (AJ). May Allāh (swt) hasten his reappearance and help us to become his true companions.

Acknowledgements

Prophet Muḥammad (s): The pen of a writer is mightier than the blood of a martyr.

True reward lies with Allāh, but we would like to sincerely thank Shaykh Salim Yusufali and Sisters Sabika Mithani, Liliana Villalvazo, Zahra Sabur, Kisae Nazar, Sarah Assaf, Nadia Dossani, Fatima Hussain, Naseem Rangwala, and Zehra Abbas. We would especially like to thank Nainava Publications for their contributions. May Allāh bless them in this world and the next.

Preface

Prophet Muḥammad (s): Nurture and raise your children in the best way. Raise them with the love of the Prophets and the Ahl al-Bayt (a).

Literature is an influential form of media that often shapes the thoughts and views of an entire generation. Therefore, in order to establish an Islamic foundation for the future generations, there is a dire need for compelling Islamic literature. Over the past several years, this need has become increasingly prevalent throughout Islamic centers and schools everywhere. Due to the growing dissonance between parents, children, society, and the teachings of Islām and the Ahl al-Bayt (a), this need has become even more pressing. Al-Kisa Foundation, along with its subsidiary, Kisa Kids Publications, was conceived in an effort to help bridge this gap with the guidance of ʿulamah and the help of educators. We would like to make this a communal effort and platform. Therefore, we sincerely welcome constructive feedback and help in any capacity.

The goal of the *Blessed Names* series is to help children form a lasting bond with the 14 Māʿṣūmīn by learning about and connecting with their names. We hope that you and your children enjoy these books and use them as a means to achieve this goal, inshāʾAllāh. We pray to Allāh to give us the strength and tawfīq to perform our duties and responsibilities.

With Duʾās,
Nabi R. Mir (Abidi)

Kisa Kids Publications
4415 Fortran Court
San Jose, CA 95134
(260) KISA-KID [547-2543]

An Introduction to the Blessed Names

Our names are a very special part of us. Many times, they shape our personalities and even explain who we are or the person we would like to become. In this series, you will explore the names and titles of our beloved 14 Ma'soomeen. Did you know that their names and titles were not just ordinary names? They were special because they were given to them by Allah!

Allah has given seven special heavenly names to our Ma'soomeen: Muhammad, Ali, Fatimah, Hasan, Husain, Ja'far, and Musa. Behind each of these names is a heavenly power!

In addition to their names, each of the Ma'soomeen also had special titles by which they became famous. Their titles were often given to them because of the circumstances of their time, but these titles and characteristics were common amongst all the Ma'soomeen. For example, Imam al-Baqir (a) was known for spreading knowledge because he was able to create many new universities and branches of knowledge during his time. However, if the other Ma'soomeen had the same opportunity, they, too, would have spread knowledge and created universities in their teaching circles. In these stories, you will discover some of the reasons why the Ma'soomeen received their specific names or titles.

Many of us share our names with these beloved Ma'soomeen or know people who do. Let's learn about these blessed names and titles so we can strive to be like our blessed Ma'soomeen!

I think as-Sadiq means...

_____

The sound of the flowing river and chirping birds echoed through the garden. Imam as-Sajjad (a) sat by the river, smelling the beautiful flowers. It was a rare sight to see the Imam (a) outside of his home since the evil caliph had guards closely watching him at all times.

On this particular day, however, the guards were busy elsewhere, so Imam as-Sajjad (a) was able to spend some time outside and enjoy the cool breeze.

Abu Khalid, a student of Imam as-Sajjad (a), knew this would be the best time to ask the Imam any questions he needed answered.

Abu Khalid quickly walked up to the Imam (a) and kissed his hand out of love and respect. He then asked for permission to ask his first question.

"O son of Rasulullah (s), who is going to be the Imam after you?" The Imam (a) pointed to a young boy playing nearby and said, "My son, Muhammad al-Baqir (a) will be the Imam after me."

Abu Khalid looked at the beautiful boy playing nearby. He was very pleased to hear this news and had many more questions for the Imam (a).

He asked, "O my Imam (a), who will be the next Imam after Imam Muhammad al-Baqir (a)?"

Imam as-Sajjad (a) replied, "The Imam after him will be named Ja'far (a)."

Still, Abu Khalid wanted to know more, and again he asked, "I want to make sure that I will be able to recognize Imam Ja'far (a)! Does he have any special titles?"

The Imam (a) nodded his head and answered, "His title is 'as-Sadiq,' meaning 'the truthful.'"

Upon hearing the word "as-Sadiq," Abu Khalid thought to himself, '*as-Sadiq' means the truthful. All the Imams (a) are truthful, so why will Ja'far (a) be the only one to be called 'truthful?'*

At first, Abu Khalid did not have the courage to ask such a question, but how could he not ask? You see, he wanted to know everything he could about Imam as-Sadiq (a)! He shyly asked, "O son of Rasulullah, all of the Imams (a) are truthful, so how come only he will be called 'as-Sadiq?'"

The Imam (a) was actually very happy, and admired Abu Khalid's curiosity.

Imam as-Sajjad (a) remembered Prophet Muhammad's answer to this very question. With a comforting smile he said, "O Abu Khalid, the Prophet (s) himself has said that Ja'far (a) should be given the title 'as-Sadiq.' He once told us that there will be another man named Ja'far who will be a liar and will claim that he is the twelfth Imam. This man will be called 'Ja'far al-Kadhaab,' which means 'Ja'far the Liar.' By calling the sixth Imam Ja'far as-Sadiq (a), everyone will be able to tell the difference between the two Ja'fars, even though they share the same first name."

Things were beginning to make sense to Abu Khalid.

Imam as-Sajjad (a) continued, "Let me explain a little more. You see, Ja'far al-Kadhaab will be friends with an evil ruler and will not accept the Imamate of Imam al-Mahdi (AJ)."

Imam as-Sajjad (a) paused for a moment and put his head down, as tears streamed down his face. He shook his head and said, "Ja'far al-Kadhaab will be related to Imam al-Mahdi (AJ) and know him very well, but he still will not accept him as the Imam."

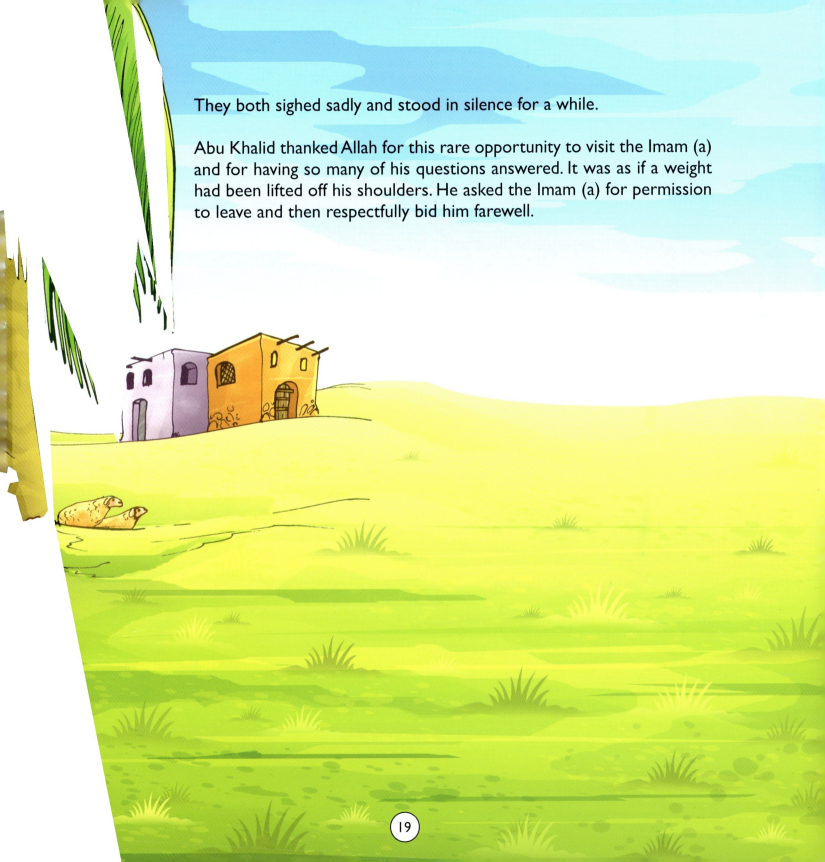

They both sighed sadly and stood in silence for a while.

Abu Khalid thanked Allah for this rare opportunity to visit the Imam (a) and for having so many of his questions answered. It was as if a weight had been lifted off his shoulders. He asked the Imam (a) for permission to leave and then respectfully bid him farewell.